Harmonizing Your Home and Extended Family

Setting Boundaries Against the Interference of Your Extended Family in Your Marriage Without Misunderstanding One Another

Adegboye S. Aduragbemi

INTRODUCTION

Marriage brings together two families, each with its customs, dynamics, and expectations, in addition to two individuals. Navigating boundaries, communication, and conflicts within the complex web of extended family relationships frequently raises concerns about upholding harmony and protecting the sacredness of the marriage bond. "Extended Family FAQ in Marriage" acts as a reference point for married couples who are trying to figure out how to handle the complications of dealing with extended family dynamics in their union.

This book contains a thorough list of frequently asked concerns, thoughtful responses, and professional guidance specific to the opportunities and challenges that come with married couples' extended family relationships. Each topic is answered with compassion, comprehension, and practical advice to help couples manage the complexities of extended family dynamics with grace and intentionality—from handling holiday get-togethers to establishing boundaries with in-laws.

"Extended Family FAQ in Marriage" provides couples with a road map for creating healthy boundaries, maintaining solid connections, and prioritizing their marriage among the challenges of extended family life through relevant tales, real-world events, and evidence-based techniques. With confidence, resiliency, and love, this book offers priceless insights and valuable skills to help you traverse the terrain of extended family relationships, whether you're combining families, negotiating cultural differences, or handling conflicts with relatives.

May you find comfort in other people's experiences that you have shared, inspiration in the knowledge of professionals, and the bravery to accept the challenges of extended family life as a means of strengthening your marriage through greater connection and fulfilment as you set out on this path of research and discovery.

Together, let's explore the ageless issues, complex relationships, and exquisite aspects of extended family dynamics in marriage.

Chapter One

Learning from other partner's experience

How disagreements between extended family members may strain

relationship

Rachel and Michael used to be a model couple in the tight-knit town of Maplewood. They had fallen madly in love when they first met in college and had aspirations of creating a happy, loving, and humorous life together. However, as they worked through the difficulties of dealing with their extended family's intricacies, their relationship started to fall apart due to competing expectations and commitments.

Rachel loved her tight relationship with her parents and siblings and was a loving nurse with a strong sense of family. She put their needs and wants above all else and respected their customs and values. Michael was a driven businessman who felt he had to live up to his family's high standards and expectations, which caused tension in his relationship with them.

Different family dynamics between Rachel and Michael initially appeared like a slight annoyance, but as they celebrated life's milestones and overcame obstacles, tensions grew. They were always at odds over things like their extended families' level of involvement in their lives, financial responsibilities, and holiday preparations. Their once-loving relationship turned into a never-ending loop of discontent, hatred, and finger-pointing.

One fateful evening, a quarrel over their annual family gathering turned into a full-blown confrontation, bringing their extended family troubles to a boiling point. Feeling conflicted about her dedication to Michael and her allegiance to her family, Rachel lost her temper and yelled at him, calling him insensitive and unsupportive. Overwhelmed and alone, Michael reacted angrily, demanding that Rachel put their relationship ahead of her family's demands.

As the years went by, there was no longer any love or connection between Rachel and Michael as their relationship continued to worsen due to their disagreements. In a last-minute determination to save their marriage, they attempted family mediation, couples therapy, and even a trial separation, but it didn't work. Ultimately, they both lamented the loss of the love they had previously experienced when they made the painful decision to separate ways.

Years later, Michael and Rachel happened to cross paths once more. They couldn't help but feel a twinge of grief for the love they had lost as they made small talk. They came to the realization that their failure to handle the intricacies of their extended family relationships had ruined their relationship, and they wished they had placed a higher value on mutual respect, communication, and compromise early on.

This narrative shows how disagreements between extended family members may strain even the most solid connections, emphasizing the value of mutual support, communication, and boundary-setting in building a strong and long-lasting alliance.

Establishing relationships through shared extended family relationships

Rachel and Michael were two people whose lives in the close-knit Willowvale community got entwined through the ties of their extended family, resulting in a partnership based on love, shared traditions, and a strong sense of belonging. Rachel, an outgoing young lady who enjoyed family get-togethers, and Michael, a good-hearted man who was firmly ingrained in his family's customs, got to know one another at a family reunion where they were celebrating their common ancestry.

They bonded with tales of their ancestors and early recollections, which made their early exchanges funny and affectionate. Michael was enthralled with Rachel's lively nature and her sincere affection for her family, while Rachel valued Michael's close relationship with his family and his commitment to upholding their customs.

As their time together grew, Rachel and Michael found a mutual respect and sense of belonging that developed into a solid and enduring bond. They accepted their responsibilities as members of their extended families, helping one another out during get-togethers, holidays, and life events and taking pleasure in the experiences they had in common that bonded them.

As they relied on one another for support and found solace and strength in their ordinary sense of family, their connection grew. The warmth and laughter of their family members filled Rachel and Michael's loving and caring home, and they treasured the relationships they had developed with each other's families.

In the presence of their relatives and extended family, Rachel and Michael exchanged vows in a moving ceremony as their love grew more assertive. They accepted their duties as family and life partners, confident that their passion and ties to their relatives would help them overcome any obstacles.

Years later, Rachel and Michael proudly and gratefully reflected on their experience. They were appreciative of the happiness and fulfilment they had found in one other and recognized that their relationship had been based on a solid foundation of love, shared values, and a strong sense of belonging to their extended families. With their family by their sides, they knew that their love would endure and thrive for many generations to come. Their link had only gotten stronger with time.

This story emphasizes the value of love, support, and connection in creating a solid and enduring partnership by showing how a relationship may be established on the basis of shared extended family relationships.

Chapter Two

Striking balance in your marriage

How can we set limits with our relatives who live far away while still keeping good relations?

Setting limits with members of your extended family requires open communication, respect for one another, and a determination to put your marriage and family first. Start by talking to your extended family members politely about your expectations and boundaries as a couple. When establishing limits, be firm yet gentle, and when needed, provide clarifications to assist people in understanding your viewpoint. Recall that a healthy balance between your connections with your own family and your extended family depends on having limits.

What should we do if we don't agree with the parenting style or lifestyle decisions made by our extended family?

Treat your extended family members with empathy, understanding, and respect for their autonomy if you disagree with the parenting style or lifestyle decisions they have chosen. Express your opinions or concerns honestly and freely, but refrain from passing judgment or levelling criticism. Rather than attempting to influence or govern the actions of others, concentrate on communicating your values and priorities. Prioritize keeping a pleasant and courteous connection with your extended family members, even if you disagree on some issues. Be prepared to agree to disagree on some things.

How can we resolve disputes or difficulties with our relatives without making things worse for our marriage?

Finding positive solutions necessitates patience, open communication, and handling disagreements or tensions with extended family members. Treat the matter as a team and give your marriage's harmony and unity priority. Discuss your worries and emotions openly with your spouse, and together, come up with ideas for how to politely and successfully handle the situation. To safeguard your marriage and well-being, be prepared to establish limits or restrict communication as needed, but also keep an open mind to forgiveness and reconciliation when it's time.

As a married couple, what part should our extended family have in our decision-making?

You and your spouse should decide how important extended family is to your decision-making process based on your own beliefs, tastes, and situation. Though it's vital to take your extended family members' opinions and suggestions into account, you and your spouse should ultimately make decisions together. Weigh the possible effects of your choices on your relationship with your extended family and be open and honest with each other about your priorities and goals. To safeguard your marriage and autonomy as a pair, be prepared to establish limits and stand your ground when needed.

How can we take care of our relationship as a couple and also spend time with our extended family?

Making conscious efforts and setting priorities is necessary to strike a balance between spending time with extended family and fostering your relationship as a spouse. Establish regular time for quality time as a pair, and be transparent about your expectations and limits when it comes to spending time with extended relatives. Prioritize your relationship with your partner, be prepared to make concessions, and come up with innovative ways to keep your relationships with your extended family intact. Recall that a robust and happy marriage depends on striking a good balance between time spent with family and time together.

What should we do if members of our extended family meddle or interfere with our personal lives or marriages?

It is crucial to swiftly and assertively handle any interference or meddling by extended family members in your marriage or personal lives. Talk to your spouse openly and sincerely about your worries and emotions. It would help if you also went about possible approaches to establishing limits and handling the circumstance well. Be stern in upholding your limits when needed, and communicate them to your extended family courteously and straightforwardly. Never forget that your first objective should always be to prioritize your connection with your partner and to safeguard the sanctity of your marriage.

How can we work with our extended family members across generational or cultural divides in a way that respects both our ancestry and our marriage?

It takes compassion, deference, and an open mind from all sides to negotiate cultural or generational divides with extended family members. When approaching the matter, show a willingness to comprehend one another's viewpoints and, if feasible, look for areas of agreement. In addition to recognizing and honouring the unique dynamics and customs inside your marriage, celebrate the depth and diversity of your background. Discuss your cultural beliefs and priorities with your partner openly and cooperatively, and together, figure out how to incorporate them into your joint existence as a couple. Recall that peace and unity in your relationships with your extended family depend on mutual respect, compromise, and a cooperative spirit.

Chapter Three

Getting it right

How can we prioritize our relationship and our family as a couple while simultaneously striking a balance with our connections with our extended family?

Prioritizing your connection as a couple, communicating, and establishing boundaries are all necessary for maintaining a healthy balance with extended family members. When it comes to time, expectations, and engagement in your lives, set clear limits with your extended family and be honest with each other about your wants and preferences. Make spending time together as a couple a priority, and make time for bonding and shared experiences that will build your relationship. To make sure that both partners feel appreciated and respected in the marriage, never forget to encourage one another to uphold appropriate boundaries with extended family members. You should also be open to reviewing and making adjustments as necessary.

What should we do when one partner wants stronger ties or more frequent contact with extended family members, but the other partner feels overburdened or worn out by them?

Effective communication within the marriage, empathy, and compromise are necessary for handling circumstances where one partner feels overburdened by encounters with extended family members. Together, create solutions that respect the needs and preferences of both partners while also acknowledging and validating each other's feelings and worries. Talk about the boundaries and expectations you have for your relationships with extended family members, and be prepared to bargain and make concessions when necessary to strike a balance that benefits you both. Prioritize helping each other feel emotionally well and fostering an atmosphere where both spouses are appreciated and understood.

How can we make sure that our ties with our extended families contribute to our overall marital happiness and well-being rather than taking away from it?

Making sure that ties with extended family improve marital satisfaction requires conscious effort, communication, and marriage boundary-setting. Make it a priority to have candid conversations with your extended family members about your boundaries and expectations for interactions with them. Work together to create explicit rules and standards for your connection with them. As a couple, be prepared to stand up for each other, convey your boundaries to members of the extended family appropriately and clearly, and encourage one another to uphold these boundaries on a regular basis. As you build a supportive environment that promotes mutual respect and understanding inside your marriage, never forget to put your relationship as partners first.

How do we respond to circumstances in which members of our extended family employ discipline methods or parenting philosophies that diverge from our own?

In order to resolve parenting style disputes within a marriage, open communication, empathy, and respect are necessary. Recognize and respect one other's emotions and worries over the disparities in parenting approaches, and engage in candid conversations regarding the potential effects of these variations on your relationships with relatives who live far away. Seek out areas of agreement that respect and appreciate the values and views of both partners and be open to learning from one another's points of view. Set a high priority on respectful and open communication. It would help if you also were proactive in settling any quarrels or misunderstandings that may occur.

How can we make sure that, even during challenging or contentious times, the ties within our extended family are solid and encouraging?

Maintaining harmonious and encouraging connections with extended family members calls for constant work, compassion, and communication within the marriage. Make it a priority to have candid conversations with your extended family members about your boundaries and expectations for interactions with them. Work together to create explicit rules and standards for your connection with them. While stating your own needs and boundaries, be prepared to listen to other family members' points of view and be willing to resolve conflicts or disagreements with them respectfully and sensitively. Even in the face of difficulties, never forget to put your partnership first and cultivate an atmosphere of support that encourages respect and understanding between you and your spouse.

How can we manage the expectations and needs of our extended family while yet preserving harmony and balance in our relationship?

Setting boundaries, communicating, and demonstrating empathy are all necessary to keep things harmonious and balanced in a marriage. Make it a priority to have frank conversations about your feelings and worries about interacting with extended family members. Work together to set up ground rules and expectations for your connection with them. As a couple, be prepared to stand up for each other, express your needs and boundaries to members of the extended family appropriately and straightforwardly, and encourage one another to uphold these boundaries continually. In addition to keeping your promises and duties to your extended family, never forget to put your partnership first and cultivate an atmosphere of mutual respect and understanding inside your marriage.

How do we respond when members of our extended family have different ideas about our roles and responsibilities within the family?

Coping with conflicting expectations calls for communication, empathy, and a determination to put your marriage as a pair first. Have frank conversations about how these discrepancies might affect your connection with extended family members, and acknowledge and affirm each other's thoughts and concerns about the expectations. As a couple, be prepared to stand up for each other, convey your boundaries to members of the extended family appropriately and clearly, and encourage one another to uphold these boundaries on a regular basis. As you build a supportive environment that promotes mutual respect and understanding inside your marriage, never forget to put your relationship as partners first.

How can we make sure that our ties with our extended families favourably impact our general well-being and happiness as a couple?

Setting boundaries, communicating, and actively participating in the marriage are all necessary to ensure beneficial contributions. Make it a priority to have candid conversations with your extended family members about your boundaries and expectations for interactions with them. Work together to create explicit rules and standards for your connection with them. As a couple, be prepared to stand up for each other, express your needs and boundaries to members of the extended family appropriately and straightforwardly, and encourage one another to uphold these boundaries continually. It's important to remember to put your marriage first and to establish a loving atmosphere that promotes respect and understanding between you and your spouse. It would be best if you also focused on building strong bonds and ties with your extended family.

Chapter Four

Setting boundaries against the extended family influence

How can we honour our duties and commitments to our extended family members while simultaneously preserving our sense of freedom and autonomy within our marriage?

Setting limits, communicating well, and being prepared to put your marriage first are all necessary to preserve independence and autonomy in your union. Discuss your unique requirements and preferences for contacts with extended family members openly and sincerely. Work together to set boundaries that respect each partner's individuality and autonomy. Be prepared to stand up for yourself when needed and respectfully and clearly express your boundaries to members of your extended family. Keep in mind to assist one another in striking a good balance between your duties and responsibilities to your extended family and your partnership.

How do we respond to circumstances in which members of our extended family meddle or unduly impact our marriage or parenting choices?

Managing interference or excessive influence from members of the extended family requires marriages to be forceful, set boundaries, and communicate well with each other. Talk to each other honestly and openly about your feelings and worries about the interference, and work together to set clear expectations and boundaries for your interactions with your extended family. As a couple, be prepared to stand up for each other and respectfully and clearly convey your boundaries to other family members. In order to express your autonomy inside your marriage and negotiate complicated family dynamics, think about getting outside aid or advice when necessary.

How can we resolve conflicts when one partner feels torn between their devotion to our marriage and their allegiance to their extended family?

Handling loyalty difficulties requires discussion, empathy, and a dedication to putting your relationship first as a pair. Talk openly and honestly about how loyalty difficulties affect your relationship, and acknowledge and affirm each other's thoughts and worries. Together, you can identify solutions that respect each partner's needs and priorities. You can also jointly set expectations and boundaries for your connection with your extended family. Remember to put your partnership's upkeep first and be willing to assist one another when it comes to standing up for your rights as a couple and setting limits with relatives.

How can we resolve disputes or conflicts that impact our family dynamics between members of our extended family and our children?

Resolving disputes between children and relatives requires sensitivity, firmness, and a dedication to standing up for your kids' rights in the marriage. Discuss your worries and emotions regarding the conflicts honestly and openly with each other. Then, work together to develop solutions that put your kids' emotional and physical safety first. As parents, you must be prepared to stand up for your children's needs and interests. You must also be willing to respectfully and clearly explain your boundaries to members of your extended family. If necessary, think about getting outside assistance or direction to help you deal with complicated family dynamics and safeguard your kids' welfare.

How do we respond when members of our extended family make uninvited comments or suggestions on our parenting style or marital status?

In a marriage, firmness, creating boundaries, and effective communication are necessary for handling unsolicited advice or criticism. Establish clear expectations and boundaries for your connection with extended family members by working together to have frank and open discussions about your feelings and worries about the interference. As a couple, be prepared to stand up for each other, convey your boundaries to members of the extended family appropriately and clearly, and encourage

28

one another to uphold these boundaries on a regular basis. As you build a supportive environment that promotes mutual respect and understanding inside your marriage, never forget to put your relationship as partners first.

How do we respond when members of our extended family meddle in our financial or personal decisions, including investments, jobs, or housing choices?

Maintaining efficient communication within the marriage, creating boundaries, and being aggressive is necessary to deal with interference in personal or financial decisions. Talk to each other honestly and openly about your feelings and worries about the interference, and work together to set clear expectations and boundaries for your interactions with your extended family. As a couple, be prepared to stand up for each other, convey your boundaries to members of the extended family appropriately and clearly, and encourage one another to uphold these boundaries on a regular basis. As you build a supportive environment that promotes mutual respect and understanding inside your marriage, never forget to put your relationship as partners first.

In particular, during holidays or special events, how can we handle expectations from extended family members regarding family get-togethers, festivities, and customs?
Managing expectations from family members who live far away requires communication, sensitivity, and a dedication to putting your marriage and your relationship first. Discuss your sentiments and worries about family get-togethers, festivities, and customs openly and sincerely with one another. Then, work together to set clear expectations and limitations for your participation in these activities. Find a balance that suits you both, and support one another in voicing your wants and preferences to relatives who are not immediate family members. It would help if you were also prepared to bargain and compromise as necessary. In the middle of family get-togethers and festivities, never forget to prioritize spending quality time together as a pair and to create opportunities for shared experiences and bonding that build your relationship.

How do we handle circumstances in which members of our extended family significantly impact our ability to make decisions, such as important life decisions or financial decisions?

Managing the influence of extended family members in a married relationship requires firmness, setting boundaries, and good communication. Discuss your worries and emotions about the impact honestly and openly with one another. Work together to set clear expectations and boundaries for your decision-making procedures. As a couple, be prepared to stand up for each other, convey your boundaries to members of the extended family appropriately and clearly, and encourage one another to uphold these boundaries on a regular basis. As you build a supportive environment that promotes mutual respect and understanding inside your marriage, never forget to put your relationship as partners first.

What should we do when members of our extended family demand that we put their wants or needs ahead of our own or our marriages?

Managing expectations in a married relationship calls for assertiveness, setting boundaries, and good communication. Together, set clear expectations and boundaries for your connection with extended family members. Be open and honest with each other about your sentiments and worries about expectations. As a couple, be prepared to stand up for each other, express your needs and boundaries to members of the extended family appropriately and straightforwardly, and encourage one another to uphold these boundaries continually. As you build a supportive environment that promotes mutual respect and understanding inside your marriage, never forget to put your relationship as partners first.

How do we respond to circumstances in which members of our extended family adhere to different societal or cultural norms that can be at odds with our morals or beliefs?

In a marriage, handling disagreements calls for compassion, deference, and open-mindedness. Regarding the differences, be upfront and honest about how they might affect your relationship with extended family members. Acknowledge and validate each other's sentiments and concerns. Seek areas of agreement that respect and honour the values and beliefs of both partners and be open to learning from each other's viewpoints and traditions. Set a high priority on respectful and open communication. It would be best if you also were proactive in resolving any disputes or misunderstandings that may occur.

Chapter Five

Extended family traditional issues

In the framework of our marriage, how do we handle arguments or problems with parents, siblings, or other relatives?

Establishing limits, having good communication skills, and treating your spouse with respect are all important when handling disagreements with your extended family. As you emphasize your relationship as a couple and recognize the value of family ties, approach these conflicts with respect and compassion. Discuss your worries and emotions honestly and openly, then work together to develop solutions that respect the needs and priorities of both parties. Be prepared to set limits as required, and if you need assistance navigating challenging family dynamics, think about getting outside support or advice.

How can we preserve our individuality and limits as a marriage while yet fostering a friendly and welcoming environment that encourages excellent connections with extended family members?

Fostering a caring and welcoming atmosphere in a married relationship requires communication, empathy, and a dedication to respect for one another. Make it a priority to have frank conversations about your expectations and boundaries when it comes to interacting with extended family. Work together to develop a mutually respectful approach that takes into consideration the requirements and preferences of both partners. To strike a balance that benefits you both, be prepared to make concessions and engage in negotiations as necessary. You should also encourage one another to uphold sound boundaries and relationships with family members who live farther away. In the midst of your relationships with extended family, never forget to put your relationship as a couple first and make time for bonding and shared experiences that will deepen your bond.

How can we resolve instances in which our extended family' differing cultures or religious beliefs could cause arguments or miscommunications?

In a married relationship, addressing cultural or religious differences across extended families calls for empathy, respect, and an open mind. Discuss openly and honestly how these differences might affect your relationship with extended family members. Respect and acknowledge each other's cultural or religious backgrounds and values. Seek areas of agreement that respect and appreciate the cultural or religious identities of both partners and be open to learning from one another's viewpoints and traditions. Set a high priority on respectful and open communication. It would help if you also were proactive in the settlement of any disagreements or misunderstandings that may occur.

In terms of parenting choices, family customs, or money problems, how can we establish appropriate boundaries with our extended family members?

Setting up appropriate boundaries in a marriage requires communication, firmness, and a dedication to putting your relationship first as a couple. Establish clear standards and expectations for your relationship with extended family members by having candid conversations with each other about your expectations and boundaries regarding interactions with them. As a couple, be prepared to stand up for each other, convey your boundaries to members of the extended family appropriately and clearly, and encourage one another to uphold these boundaries on a regular basis. As you build a supportive environment that promotes mutual respect and understanding inside your marriage, never forget to put your relationship as partners first.

How can we deal with the difficulties that come with having blended families, especially when it comes to reintegrating relatives from past relationships?

Managing blended families calls for patience, understanding, and honest communication between the couple. Discuss with an open mind and honestly each of your expectations and boundaries with your partner, and acknowledge and affirm each other's thoughts and worries about integrating extended family members from prior relationships. Work together to identify solutions that respect the needs of both partners and put the welfare of all family members first in order to negotiate the unique difficulties and dynamics of blended families successfully. Be prepared to look outside for assistance or direction when necessary. Additionally, give top priority to establishing a welcoming and inclusive atmosphere that encourages respect and understanding between all family members.

While keeping appropriate boundaries, how can we help our kids develop good connections with grandparents, aunts, uncles, and other relatives?

Promoting healthy connections between children and members of the extended family calls for communication, empathy, and a determination to put the needs of the whole family first within the marriage. Give kids a chance to connect and bond with their extended family members by providing them with quality time, but also set clear expectations and boundaries for these relationships. Be prepared to discuss parenting choices and preferences honestly and openly with members of your extended family. Work together to build a welcoming and inclusive atmosphere that values and respects the roles that each spouse plays in the family.

How do we respond when members of our extended family follow customs or cultures that are at odds with our values or beliefs?

In order to resolve issues arising from cultural or lifestyle disparities within a marriage, empathy, respect, and an open mind are necessary. Regarding the differences, be upfront and honest about how they might affect your relationship with extended family members. Acknowledge and validate each other's sentiments and concerns. Seek areas of agreement that respect and honour the values and beliefs of both partners and be open to learning from each other's viewpoints and traditions. Set a high priority on respectful and open communication. It would help if you also were proactive in settling any disputes or misunderstandings that may arise.

About the Author

ADEGBOYE S. ADURAGBEMI is a manager, business administrator, entrepreneur, and motivational speaker in Africa. ADEGBOYE has his BA from Yale University, IPMA from Adonai University, and a Masters in Business Administration (MBA) from the University of Salford, Manchester.

He was born in South Africa but is presently based in Nigeria as a motivational speaker and marriage counsellor in institutions, sectors, and seminars with young and upcoming managers all over Africa.

Acknowledgements

I want to express my sincere gratitude to everyone who helped with the "FAQ on Communication in Marriage." Throughout this journey, their encouragement, insight, and support have been priceless.

I want to start by acknowledging the fact that, without God, this guide wouldn't have been possibly achieved.

And also to my spouse, who has always been motivating and supportive in making this task successful, I will always love and appreciate you.

I have many couples to appreciate who have shared their experiences, challenges, and victories with me over the years. Your openness, weakness, and tenacity have enhanced the book's pages and provided priceless insights into the difficulties of marriage communication.

My sincere gratitude goes out to my family and friends for their continuous support and encouragement during this journey. Your wise advice, tolerance, and words of support have helped me get through the complicated process of writing and releasing this book.

I sincerely thank the specialists and experts who have so kindly offered their knowledge and skills in marriage and communication. Your advice and thoughts have improved this book's quality and depth, and I really appreciate your contributions.

Finally, I would like to express my profound gratitude to all of the readers of this work. As you journey through the process of communication in your marriage, I hope that the knowledge, direction, and encouragement provided within these pages will be a source of inspiration and empowerment for you. I sincerely appreciate your help.

www.ingramcontent.com/pod-product-compliance
Lightning Source LLC
Chambersburg PA
CBHW051249120626
46547CB00014B/1866